One Rupee Film Diaries: A Brief History of Dime

(Part 1)

ANAMITRA ROY

DEDICATION

Tutu,
The little street-dog
Who stayed with me
For a few days
When I was six

CONTENTS

ACKNOWLEDGMENTS

Members and supporters of Little Fish Eat Big Fish, our no-budget filmmakers' forum, without you this book won't have been possible! Thanks a lot for being there in the time of need…

1 WHY DIME

The names of the chapters might make it seem that the book is very well-planned. Well, it is not. This book probably did not need any chapter division. I never self-published a book before, I mean, of course I did, but not in this language. Had this been a Bengali book, I won't have given a damn about the format. But, as I already said, I never published a book in English before, or, as a matter of fact, I never even tried to write anything constructive in this language. Couple of years ago, I translated 4 of my poetry (or anti-poetry, whatever it is) in English. That was my only effort. So, when I realized that even my writing or what I have to say might be of interest to some people (unfortunately, I'm unable to locate) I also realized that these people can be from any origin and they can absolutely be speaking any language. So, this time, Bengali wasn't enough. In fact, one of the reasons that I could not limit myself into writing and just writing is that Bengali wasn't enough. Often, it is the 2nd language of the people who actually have some extra bucks to spend on literature, music, film etc. I'm not talking about popular stuff here of course. Everyone, almost everyone has money to spend for Salman Khan or Sachin Tendulkar, that's not the point. People who might be interested in an alternative literature or any kind of alternative stream of art often relate to English in a better way than Bengali. Not that I'm talking about the other communities in India, this is even true for Bengal itself. And, I'm afraid; it's becoming even truer every day.

So, where were we? --- yes, when I realized that I shall write something in

English now, the first question that came to my mind was, of course, who is going to publish it? It's my job to write, no one else can write what I have to write, that's fair enough but it just cannot be my job to knock publishers with a manuscript in my hand. I never did that for a single piece I wrote in my life. So, amazon was the fittest option. Now when I visited the site they offered me guidance through the whole process. I was happy and I got this word template with acknowledgement and chapter division and blah blah blah! This whole thing confused me like hell. So, I just took my diary (the real one on which you have to write with a pen), made a plan how to write and what's there to write etc and came back to my desk. I thought it would be good to explain (not to anyone else but to myself) that why even I should write. It has always been important for me to enjoy whatever I'm doing. As I'm writing this, I don't even know if anyone is out there to read or who's reading. So, automatically it becomes important that all these writings serve a purpose in my life. I am not that kind of a megalomaniac to think that this shall end all my pain and agony and maybe I'll become very popular and raise all the money still needed for the film just by writing. In fact, I'm kind of pessimist. Right now I'm thinking that no one ever is going to read this book so I must discover a reason to keep on writing.

All the blasphemous things I have done till date, there was only one reason. I have always tried to rediscover myself. When you are not doing anything that helps you earn money (as if that's the only thing we are born to do) it becomes a psychological need; asking yourself, "God, why did I do that" or, "Damn! What on earth am I doing" and being able to find an answer. It's like relocating or re-situating yourself and rediscovering your relationship with everything on the planet. There are other beings like me across the world I believe and if you are not one of us, believe me; it takes a lot to keep on fighting like this. Even this morning someone asked me, an old acquaintance, "did you get a job"? I told him, as I always tell everyone (the honest most answer I think), "I'm working on my own. So, I'm not looking for a job like others do." Normally, they don't ask anything else after this. There is a great creator inside you whom nobody recognizes and that great sage just doesn't allow you to go to the market and do some striptease to earn money; well, you cannot tell that to everyone. People know that you are a writer, but they never get to read any of your writings in the popular dailies or monthlies. People know that you are a filmmaker, but they don't know how to get to watch a film of yours. And if you start telling them about the philosopher inside you who has a theory that the industry is this and the industry is that, people will just make faces and pretend that they understood everything you said and end up saying, "at the end of the day, money is important"! So, let's not go to that extent. Let the mist be there. No one is going to ask you about your current bank balance so hopefully you'll save yourself from lying.

Now, let's get back to the context. This book is not planned. I was writing something in Bengali in some webzine when I realized that some people might find interest in what I have to share. And these people may be from any origin, they may hail from any place in the world. That's what pushed me to writing these diaries. What happened next, I have shared earlier. You must have already noticed that there's no forward or preface in this book. It's because there was no space for that kind of a thing in this template. So, I just made no effort to include one. Also, I have this feeling every time that whatever I'm writing or making is like a forward to my next work. These diaries can also be interpreted as forwards to the film which is yet to find a release. Now, why this brief history of dime? For the last couple of years, I've been working like hell. I had to talk too much every day. I had to talk so much that I feel my brain cells got kind of shattered. It took 474 days to raise 285K INR for our film, Aashmani Jawaharat aka Diamonds in the sky which is widely known as the 0ne Rupee Film Project. Along with Sriparna (my wife and co-activist and co-visionary and I don't know how else to put it), I was raising funds, writing script, writing promotional stuff, acting, thinking about the camera angle, rehearsing with co-actors and going through hours of footages and arranging locations and sets and calling the driver and seeing to how to manage the lunch for the unit......................that bad feeling is already coming back to me as I'm writing all these. So, I won't write any more about what all I just had to do. You can guess the life of a DIY filmmaker.

Basically, for me, writing this book is like after uncounted days of fever, sitting by the river and recapitulating where I was, what I was doing and through this process discovering where I am now. As I look back, 19th February, 2012, I was in a train. It was a chair car and me, Sriparna, my mother and Sriparna's mother, we were going to Puri, Odisha. Me and Sriparna, we were going to attend Bring Your Own Film Festival. My mother was going because she had to meet an old colleague for some job related reasons and since she was going we asked Sriparna's mother to join us. Puri is a nice place. You can only get healthier by spending a week there. So, that's how the team was formed. Now these chair car coaches in Shatabdi express, they have 2+3 sitting system. All the three ladies sat on one side and I had to sit beside a stranger, an aged guy. Through the course of the journey, I discovered that my aged fellow is kind of a talkative guy as he kept on asking me this and that about my life and what I am doing in this train, why did I even board it etc. I'm not that talkative generally. When it comes to interacting with strangers I am a good listener. Gradually I came to know a lot about this guy, my fellow passenger. He hails from Patna, Bihar. He used to be an officer of higher ranks in Coal India. His name is Mr. Abhayanand Pathak. His residence in Patna is named Anand Bhawan. He is a poet and he has got two books to his credit, one is *Sparsh* (Touch) and the other one Ehsaas (Feel/Sensing). Also, he is one of the maternal uncles of Mr. Vinay Pathak, the reputed actor. He is a vegetarian and a Brahmin. The list of what all I came to know just doesn't end. I was becoming quite fond of his rhetorical talking. It was full of poetic wisdom. Now, Mr. A. N Pathak, where I liked this man the most is that he told me never to care about money. It just keeps on coming and going. Let it be like that. One shall keep on doing what he or she is destined to do. This statement kind of matches my perspective. So, now he got the whole of me. We just kept on talking for the rest of the journey.

Around 10:30 that night, we reached Chakratirtha House in Puri. I was still thinking about what all Mr. A.N Pathak had told me during the journey. There was a story (or an incident rather) that dates back to the 90s. Mr. Pathak was at Kurla railway station (now known as Lokamanya Tilak Terminus). It was daytime. There was another guy with him from the office to see him off. The train was delayed by a couple of hours. So, they were resting in the waiting room. Suddenly a man, evidently younger, came in and approached the other guy, "Sir, can you please give me one rupee"? The other guy replied in a rude manner, "Why don't you get a job instead"? The man left without saying a single word and approached another guy sitting nearby. Mr. Pathak got interested in this fundraiser. He was not a conventional beggar, the young guy asking one rupee from everyone. He was in formal attire, white shirt and black trouser and he approached almost all the people, surprisingly, in English. So, as soon as this guy left the waiting room Mr. Pathak followed him. After observing him for ten minutes or so, now he approached the guy and gave him one rupee. He also asked the reason of his begging. The reply was quite unusual. Mr. Pathak came to know that this fundraiser of ours belongs to a not-so-well-to-do family. He is a graduate of commerce but he wants to become a writer. He has a manuscript ready. It's a novel but he could not find a good deal from any publisher in the city. So, now he is planning to publish it himself, but, he has no money. So, he is raising funds this way.

I was thinking, if he could, why can't we?

2 WHAT'S DIME

"If At First the Idea Is Not Absurd, Then There Is No Hope for It"

As I'm looking back, I'm trying to figure out how it all happened! What kicked me, where and how, to just jump on something, some concept! We are talking about February, 2012, when it all started. I think the experiences we had at BYOFF, 2011 has something to do with it. That was the first time we attended BYOFF. We had heard about it previously, but not much. All we knew was like this is a hierarchy-less film festival. Anyone can just hop in with their film, better, not only films, just anything. A lot of independent minded off-the-track kinds of people gather in Puri every year in February from 21st to 25th. In January, 2011, our second compilation of no-budget fiction films came out. We never aimed big with our films. The main reason was lack of money. We were trying to develop a language, an aesthetic of money-less film. We knew only a hierarchy-less film festival would agree to screen our films. That was the only reason BYOFF attracted us. As usual, we had no money. The 10k that we raised by selling the DVDs in Little Magazine Fair and Kolkata International Book Fair came in handy. I was the curator; I had to take the decision. I thought this would be best use of the money; me and Sriparna, we would go and attend BYOFF and screen all the short films there. My decision seemed to be perfect when I got a message from Gurpal Singh, the reputed actor and one of the organizers (the most vocal guy in whole BYOFF). While I was yet to make

6

a final decision I put a status on Facebook, "If money is phallus I feel castrated. Not going to be able to attend BYOFF". Within 10 minutes I got a message from Gurpal, "Just come. Money is no big deal. We'll see to it together".

And the decision was made!

We thought this is going to be our kind of festival. All the people will be great! But utopia is just utopia and cannot turn into reality. At that point of time I was a bit interested about Q (Mr. Qaushiq Mukherjee of Gandu fame). I was interacting with him, trying to figure out his purpose and standpoint. Although I did not watch any of his films, I had a feeling whatever he is, he is an alternative to the whole crap the film industry produces. We are coming back to him shortly.

So, we were in BYOFF. We registered all the films for screening. We could not register Abhishek Bhattacharya's *Memories_alternate cut* as no one from the crew was available to present the film. No problem! We got three consecutive slots on 24th Februray, 2011 in the post-dinner session. On the morning of 24th, Gurpal gives me a call, "Anamitra, can you come to Pink House now? I have something important to discuss". In an hour, I was in Pink House, talking to Gurpal from whom I came to know that Mr. Q has reached that morning with his team direct from Berlin and he has expressed wish to screen his film at the earliest. Now, there's this 61 minute slot scheduled for my film *Secret Footage* which can be replaced with *Gandu* if I agree. Otherwise, the organizers would have to talk to 3 short filmmakers at least to get a slot long enough for *Gandu*. If I agree, my film would get a decent slot in exchange on the closing day for sure. I was in good terms with the maker. Also, I had a fair idea of the craze *Gandu* had already created. I didn't want to get sandwiched. I left the slot and didn't even ask why they call it a hierarchy-less film festival and why they say that slots are provided on a first-come-first-serve basis. These questions, at that time, didn't even come to my mind since I was apparently in good terms with Mr. Q

So, contrary to the popular idea that *Gandu* was screened publicly in India for the first time at the Osian's Cinefan Film Festival held in August 2012, the film was actually screened at BYOFF on 24th February, 2012 in the post-dinner session just after Sriparna's short film *Two or Three Things about Visuals,* exactly the slot that was meant for *Secret Footage* made by me and my dear friend Mr. Snigdhendu Bhattacharya. I remember Gurpal saying that Q has said that he thinks only BYOFF is this kind of a festival in India that would not be afraid to screen a film like *Gandu* etc and blah blah blah! What happened after the screening or what happened between me and Mr. Q, I won't write that here. I would rather write about what happened to *Secret Footage*, the film. I got the closing slot of the festival. I was happy with that because I thought there would be a lot of people to watch my film. Actually I did not have any idea about the BYOFF crowd. Initially, *Secret Footage,* which is a docu-fiction, was introduced as a thriller. I tried to manage it while I presented the film but it was of no use. Of course this one is the worst film I have ever made, in fact I make bad films only, but I do make Films at least, and I make it in such a situation I would like to see some big shots put themselves in my shoes and try. Now, there was this character in BYOFF, Viraj Singh, a cinematographer who was in the mood for party. He seems to be a little irritable and a little overdrunk always but a good guy otherwise, I don't know why, as soon as my film reached 12 minutes he lit up the closing bonfire. We had a crowd of around 150. All of them left, almost. The party began. My film was still being screened for 15 people or so. I got up from the chair found out Gurpal Singh and asked him to turn off the projector. I was in no mood to screen my film. He said, "No, let it play. At least some people are watching".

After a point of time, I was laughing! It was pure irony. Footage from a people's court in Lalgarh was being played on the screen and there was a people's party going on around the screening tent. When the screening ended and lights were turned on, I found a total number of 22 people in and around the tent. The party was still on.

In 2012, financially, I was in a better condition. But the 15k or 20k I spent out of my pocket just to attend BYOFF, I wanted to put that to some use. Of course, I was in no mood for networking with frustrated people looking for an all-night-long party on some cool sea-beach in eastern India. Also, by that time I had come across some real big guys, like a commandant running a whole regiment, I mean, not some megalomaniac doing nothing and being judgmental and considering his/her own contribution to the society to be of great worth. I was not that kid out of some small town in Bengal anymore. I had fair idea of things like client, market etc. Also, I had this power of finding out more or less who is what by interacting 5 minutes with anyone, like who's the real rebel and who's just posing, who's an artist and who's the merchant etc. We were back at BYOFF and the reason was apart from all the idiots, the fest also brought us in touch with some good guys. One of them was Surja Shankar Dash, an activist filmmaker based in Bhubaneswar. So, just after reaching Chakratirtha House, I called Surja. He was taking a walk and talking to Gurpal. He said, they are coming to Pink House. I said, ok, we'll meet on the way.

Let's get back to 2010. In the month of May, my M.A course was over. All of a sudden I got my much desired freedom. I had a lot of time. So, I started approaching different people with a script. It was a gangster thriller, but a bit different than what you normally see in works of this genre. A reference to that script and that phase can be found in Aashmani Jawaharat. Gradually, I was realizing that the world is just-too-much-not-like-me and getting depressed. At this time, one night, me and Sriparna, we discussed about the possible ways to come up with a feature. There was another weird script in my mind, *Vulgar E.T*, a sci-fi. We made a list of people who could possibly give us money if we really start raising funds for a feature film. We found that raising 175 grand (INR) won't be a big deal really. So, the idea of crowd-funding was already there.

And the A.N Pathak chapter already did take place

Now, we were in front of Surja and Gurpal. We hugged each other and the first thing came out of my mouth was, "Gurpal ji, I want to make a crowd-funded feature-length docu-fiction and I want to start the fundraising campaign at BYOFF this year! We'll approach everyone we come across and ask for money for the film. Even a contribution as minimum as one rupee is welcome. We are going to call this campaign the One Rupee Film Project. Can we count on your support"?

Gurpal said, "But a lot of people have actually tried that. They all ended up wasting that money for fags and boozes. Why would people believe you? Why should they trust you"?

I said, "we'll start only after our films are screened"! It didn't seem convincing enough.

That night, I opened up the official blog of the One rupee film project and the next morning we took a print out of a page with 16 impressions. We Xeroxed the page, 50 copies and we cut it into small coupons containing the blog's URL, my phone number, our forum's email id etc.

On the closing day, the 25th, the campaign began officially, that is to say, we turned into humble but desperate beggars!

3 WHO'S DIME

Dimes are what constitute the rupee. Rupee is the whole collage and dimes are the bits and pieces used in its composition. These can be the people, the forces, the reasoning, the ideologies, the blockades and everything else that have contributed to the physicality of the rupee or its existence in the conceptual plane.

As I said earlier, chapter division was not really needed for this book. All I'm doing here is discussing different things about the dime. We come from a very unusual background. We shouldn't have been making films at all; I mean, no one in our position would have come this way. Had they come, they would have been here for business and only business. We don't belong to a mass movement either. We are dwelling somewhere between these two, the corporate world and the reality of mass resistance. Let's not be hypocrites and pose as revolutionaries. We are gray; we belong to both of these. We come to know of some resistance happened somewhere in some far-off land through media houses' websites. We cannot ignore any of them, the resistance or the media house. They are there and their existence does not depend on our essentialist belief systems. If we ignore them, that's probably because we are not seeing properly or just seeing but not getting it.

When I met Sriparna in 2005, I was trying to come up with a little magazine with a couple of guys from the school. It was only for good that the magazine had not been published till then. We were confused. There were three or four roads, with evident differences, lying ahead of us. Basically we

11

were still debating on what should be the character of the magazine. Whether it should be something conventional, or something hardcore Marxist in nature, or something completely different from these two; we were yet to make up our minds. What should be the perfect approach or the outlook, we were still searching. We had a lot of contradictions within ourselves. Three of us were from three different backgrounds. The only common factor was that all the three were born and brought up in financially middle-class families, I mean, at that time what we thought to be the class dwelling between the rich and the poor. Later on, I discovered different shades and realized we were more or less only a bit wealthier than what normally is called poor. It would be more of a stylized statement to call ourselves belonging from the middle-class after all the shades of middle-class I have seen in different cities including Kolkata. These two closest pals of mine, one of them was raised in a joint family, his father used to work in a jute-mill and the other one used to stay with his parents in a house where his maternal uncle and aunt also used to stay, his father was a senior engineer working for a big name in the realty estate trade. My mother, she was a teacher teaching in a govt. sponsored school (she is still in that job) and my father used to work in the purchase department of a private concern till it was shut down in 1997. In the year '97, I was in the 5th standard and the time I'm talking about right now is 2005 when I was trying to find my own voice. Sriparna joined us. Her father runs his own business of building houses etc. With this new presence of the significant other in my life my quest got a new push. The search of own identity, so to speak, was   accelerated   for   better.

After two failed efforts, finally our magazine (***Byas, 1st issue with a special segment on anti-establishment in Bengali literature***) was published in February, 2007. May be some other day, I'll come back with those stories. It was a hell of a time. The mass movement against the state government's land acquisition policy had begun. We were, of course, with the people. There were lots of things happening all around. I don't know why, there must be a blockade; every time I start speaking about this period of my life, I don't feel like speaking at all. But, in short, some important incidents took place that left their impressions and effects on me forever. I never met any serious faker before this time. I never had an idea that there can be some people on earth who just talk and do nothing. I never knew that most of the living stalwarts of alternative Bengali literature are also politicians looking to create their own colonies of yes-men. Not today, but someday I may come back with these stories.

One of the most important incidents that helped me get a fair idea of what the world is like took place on the evening of 8th December, 2006. It was the last day of the govt. sponsored poetry festival. We were distributing leaflets in protest. Also, we were campaigning with posters for a convention on acquisition of agricultural land, industrialization and state repression. We could already smell something wrong after the massive lathicharge on protesters in Singur on 2nd December, 2006. On the 8th itself, journalists were beaten badly by some policemen in my district. We were not ready to accept this situation at all. And the so-called intellectuals of Kolkata, who would come out and hold rallies and would boycott the film festival next year, they were still sleeping. In fact, I'm sure, some of them were there in that poetry festival, clapping after hearing poetry on what happened in Manipur or some stuff like that! I got pulled in by Kolkata police from Ravindra Sadan complex along with a friend of mine for being too much active on my own. We were taken to the Hastings P.S. Thanks to the police, the convention was largely successful. Of course, some revolutionaries like Mr. Suman Mukhopadhyay (the filmmaker) did not have time to attend. It feels strange when someone you respect breaks a promise in a hilarious way. On the day of the convention, Mr. Mukhopadhyay said he is on his way at around 16:30 hours. At 17:00 hours, he told me that he is unable to find the venue. From 17:30 hours, some drunkard started receiving my calls (I was calling him on his cellphone) and kept on telling me that Mr. Mukhopadhay has mistakenly left without his cellphone. After that day, I deleted his number. I had to delete a lot of numbers in the coming years for different reasons, some equally surreal like this one. Anyway, the big shots had the next year for their street-shows.

Why do some people only speak up after some people had died?

None of my business really! I was a kid, a little-magazine activist only. No one was feeding me anyway, so, I had no real reason to worry about things like what if the ruling party changes all of a sudden. Situation was not the same for everyone, I can understand. But only now I do understand. I did not know about the world or the people in it. Thanks to all these that gave me the eye. One amusing thing I came to know very recently is that Surja Shankar was in Kolkata at that time. He also used to hang around Ravindra Sadan Complex. But, we didn't know each other. It seems funny! Thanks to BYOFF again!

After Kolkata International Book Fair, 2007 I opted for a kind of self-exile. In our apartment, we have an isolated room on the rooftop beneath the water reservoir. This room was not in the original plan of the building. But the space came out somehow due to mal-execution. I kind of locked myself up in the room and kept on thinking and writing. At this point of time, except meeting my parents and my sisters daily during dinner-time, I was in touch with two human beings only. One of them was one of the guys from school, Mr. Snigdhendu Bhattacharya and of course, my significant other, Sriparna. Sometimes I used to go to the college too as I was a student of 2nd year already, but nothing interesting I could find there. So, these two avenues of communication were open, one a maverick guy who thinks and writes a lot of unusual stuff and the other a woman hard to define who had severe unbelievable skills with things like paintbrush and a pencil or a pen. The old team was not there anymore. The friend I used to stay in Kolkata with was in a rehab. The other friend from the school whom I began with left the team for personal reasons. The combination of this three still in touch, gave birth to an unprinted literary bulletin (**Byas Khasra Sankhya**) with collages, cut-ups, alternative poetry and prose. We Xeroxed and distributed it in some small town little-magazine fairs. Since I my love relationship with Sriparna was becoming condensed, Snigdhendu, by this time, started to feel a bit left alone. We were working together in the field of literature like previous days, but there were new contradictions between us now. These contradictions, however, were probably the reason behind two collections of poems, one by me and one by Snigdhendu, same in the form but different content-wise. My collection (**Shabdoprokriyakoron**) was self-published in book fair 2008. It was similar to the previous literary bulletin I mentioned, unprinted, full of cut-ups, Xeroxed to distribute. The collection was mostly self-illustrated except that there was a unique piece of art, painting, that is to say, made by Sriparna in each copy. One month later, Snigdhendu came up with his collection (**Nijoswo Protirodh**) in the same format. It was all done by him, but there were no paintings. He didn't even ask Sriparna.

14

We had already made up our minds that we are not going to turn **Byas** into an institution like publishing house or something. So, in 2009, we did not use the name, but did publish another bulletin (**Manik Bandopadhyay Sarani or Randhanshala**). But before that, it was still 2008, when I got a call from Mr. Arupratan Ghosh. It was the same year, we three (me, Sriparna and Snigdhendu) had already started making our first independent short film. It was meant to be a docu-fiction on the life and works of Subimal Mishra, the maverick anti-establishment author (**Subimal Mishra: Shot at Underground/ Roughcut: Subimal**), which we could not complete and dropped after a couple of years. The author himself wanted a biopic. He was not getting what we had in mind. So, after two-or three shoots he was not co-operating at all. Anyway, let's get back to Mr. Ghosh. He called me just to verify that Anamitra Roy, the name of the poet as found on **Shabdoprokriyakoron**, exists for real. When he found out that not only Anamitra, but Sriparna and Snigdhendu (he wrote a preface for my collection) also does exist, he expressed wish to meet in person. Amitava Praharaj and Arupratan Ghosh are undoubtedly two names amongst the most famous alternative poets of the generation just a decade senior to us. We were really close friends with Amitava (popularly known as Baby). We used to stay at his place in Narendrapur sometimes. If you are not one from this alternative Bengali literature circle, you cannot even imagine Amitava's popularity. His nickname "Baby" had successfully coined a word, "babism" (baby + ism), which basically means drinking too much and roaming on the streets without senses and getting arrested over and over again. In the summer of 2008, I was already a graduate and I joined Jadavpur University to pursue a master degree in film studies. This was totally against my wish. I wished to become a copywriter in some advt. agency. Baby was a creative director working for two such agencies in Kolkata at the same time. I had also talked to him. But my parents wanted me to go for higher studies. They made a quite political move. When they failed to convince me they convinced Sriparna to convince me. And I was convinced (but not quite)!

Within a couple of months of getting the call from Arupratan, I went to meet him. We met at a country-liquor-pub, got quite equally impressed by each other and talked for three hours at least. I came to know about his writings and his efforts in filmmaking. He also came to know about our new effort of making the docu-fiction on Subimal Mishra with a MiniDV Handycam that Sriparna owns. The final output of that meeting was this decision --- we would make a film together. Arupratan would write it and direct it; I would act in it as well as edit it and the film would be made with Sriparna's camera (later, she also had to act in it). That was the beginning of the Kolkata No-Budget chapter, as well as the seed of **Little Fish Eat Big Fish**, our no-budget filmmakers' forum.

Within a couple of weeks, the film was made. For me, it was not a good film, but this much at least was proved that we can actually make a film for 500 or 600 rupees (10 USD). Friends who watched the film were encouraged. They had their own films in mind and now means were available. Let's not go into the quality of the films, different people would have different opinions, but the effort was certainly significant. Around 35 people participated in the making of 5 short fictions. 31st January, 2010, at Kolkata International Book Fair, **Five No Budget Films**, a compilation consisting of these efforts, was released on DVDs and the edition was out of stock within seven days. There was no involvement of the film industry. There was no corporate funding or whatever.

In India, I don't know, if anything like this had ever happened before!

ABOUT THE AUTHOR

This was there in the template. I could attach my photograph here of course, or write about my academic qualification, but instead, I thought of using this space as a post-script. Until and unless we get completion funds, we have decided to lock the film up in the cold storage. I'll be writing two more volumes of this diary. Till then I'll wait and see. I'm expecting people to come forward and support us and at the same time I'm also not expecting anyone to do so. That's because our film, I feel, does not have sell-ability in that sense. So, houses, as such, I don't think would stand by our initiative. They are in the market for business and only business undoubtedly. But if you think you are independent, should you really give a damn about what goes in the market? We don't expect anything from them. But of course, we believe, there are people who would love to watch it. Hopefully, these writings would serve the appetite, that we could create, not get killed with time!

www.ingramcontent.com/pod-product-compliance
Lightning Source LLC
Chambersburg PA
CBHW021417170526
45164CB00002B/692